Contents

DID YOU KNOW?

For parents and children accustomed to long, time-consuming tests, it may seem impossible to truly gather sufficient placement information with just a few questions. But, the truth is that you can easily and effectively learn where to place your child academically in a subject with just twenty simple questions!

How is this possible? Well, keep in mind that most achievement tests are administered to large groups of students, and the results are processed through computers. Therefore, these tests require a minimum of three to five questions per topic in order to assess an average.

When a test is administered one on one and the parent walks through each question with their child, however, the assessment results are not strictly based on right or wrong answers. Instead, they are based on observation of thought processes, understanding of the question, and the ability to work through the question or problem. As a result, typically only one question, combined with interactive administration of the test, is required to adequately assess a child's level of understanding.

Well Planned Start includes both the administrator guide and step-by-step answer key in order for parents to confidently administer, observe, and evaluate the test-taking process to understand exactly where their children place.

A TOOL FOR PARENTS

As a mom of five, I began giving my kids achievement tests at an early age. After teaching them how to fill in the small circles and sharpen their number 2 pencils, the kids would walk into classrooms, doors would close, and testing would begin. Six weeks later, I would receive test reports which gave vague indications of how each child was doing compared to children across the nation. The broad descriptions of achievement in specific areas provided very little useful information to help me know how to strengthen my kids in the coming year.

Over the years, I sought an assessment option that would help me choose the best curriculum, cover information unknown to my child, and fill in any educational gaps. Unfortunately, none of the tests I found accomplished this goal. That needed to change!

Recognizing the need, I began working with the Well Planned Gal curriculum developer **Tiffany Orthman, M.Ed.** to develop a one-of-a-kind, easy-to-use assessment and placement test for parents and children to work through together.

Well Planned Start is unique as it guides you, the parent, to a better understanding of what your child knows, comprehends, and can process correctly. This educational evaluation tool offers a two-sided assessment. First, you will find a parent assessment, helping you discover what you know about your child. Second, a student placement test walks your child through a series of questions while you follow along with an administrator guide that helps you know how to process your child's answers and thinking processes.

Best of all, I've included helpful tips for each of the subjects and areas, as well as a checklist of milestones for this school year. Milestones work as a guide as you watch your child develop emotionally, physically, and educationally throughout the year.

As you proceed through this book and into your school year, remember these five key points:

- Relax! This is not a comparison or a judgment game. This is a tool to help you determine where your child is.

- Use the information to make improvements. Spend extra time or use a different approach where there are weaknesses. Offer more activities if you need to challenge your child. If you have not covered an area, now is the time!

- Try to set aside presuppositions as you begin the assessment. Remember, dislike for a subject does not indicate a weakness.

- These assessments are based on grasping concepts rather than parroting correct answers.

- Bible has been added as an additional component in these assessments. Keep in mind, though, that spiritual growth is not based on age. This is simply a resource to help you have an idea of where to look for and encourage growth.

Rebecca Farris
WELL PLANNED GAL

BOOK OVERVIEW

The Well Planned Start has been organized and arranged in order of sequence. Each section has an introduction with detailed information on how to assess your child, administer the placement test, and understand the milestones.

PARENT ASSESSMENT TESTS

The goal of this section is to become familiar with what your child knows. If your child has been attending school or hybrid homeschooling, this area will give you the opportunity to begin dialogues to understand the depth of understanding in each subject.

There are detailed instructions on how to use this assessment, as well as worksheets to journal your findings. At the end of this section, we give practical teaching tips to help you enhance each subject area.

STUDENT PLACEMENT TESTS

Unlike standardized testing, these placement tests allow parents to see first hand the specific areas children excel and need help in. By using the guide to administer the tests, you not only give instructions to your child, but you will also follow instructions that help you know what to watch for as the child works through the questions. This allows you to discover where the breakdown begins in the process.

PARENT TEACHING TIPS

After administering tests, you will find practical teaching tips and activity suggestions for every concept covered in the placement test. Use these suggested activities to strengthen low-scoring areas, keep your child challenged, fill in gaps, and more!

KINDERGARTEN MILESTONES

Complete with a checklist of milestones, Well Planned Start provides a year-long guide on what to expect from your child physically, emotionally, and academically. Beyond what they should achieve, we've included what they may achieve, including even advanced achievements. An additional checklist is included in each area to let you know how to help your child along the way.

TESTING OBSTACLES

If your child has never taken a test before or has trouble when testing, the Well Planned Start assessments offer a great introduction to testing and are relaxed enough to put any child at ease.

The assessments are not timed, and there are no little circles on separate sheets of paper that children have to navigate. Instead, parents are encouraged to engage children, review instructions, or stop for a break when needed.

In the comfort of your home and with the assurance of a parent administering the assessment, children working through Well Planned Start are able to relax, comprehend, access the information, and enjoy the experience.

Well Planned Start ensures an accurate and enjoyable assessment and placement for children and parents.

#1 START HERE

Begin with the Parent Assessment

PARENT ASSESSMENT

The following pages contain the parent assessment tests for math, language arts, history & geography, science, and Bible. Use this section to begin understanding what your child should know and comprehend. Here are a few tips as you proceed through the questions ahead:

- If you are unsure about the questions and answers, do a quick Internet search.

- If you are unsure whether a topic has been or will be covered, do a little digging. Speak to a representative at your child's previous school or take a quick look through your past or current homeschool curriculum.

- Engage your child in a discussion to see how deep his or her knowledge is. Remembering the significance of an event is more important than knowing a date for a test.

- Try to figure things out together. This is a team effort.

- Lack of information does not necessarily indicate a gap. For example, if you have not covered early American history yet but are sure your child would understand it, give your child credit for abilities.

- Watch your child's general attitude toward learning. If there is a lot of negativity, plan to take a step back to regain a love of learning.

- As you process through this assessment with your child, go with your gut instinct. If you feel your child is good at something, say so. If you feel he or she is struggling, say so.

- Think back to all the times you observed your child doing school work, playing, or having conversations. Do you feel that he or she understands the concepts?

- If you don't feel confident in your knowledge, ask for help from family and friends.

- Ask classmates, former teachers, or other homeschool moms what their observations of your child are.

- Be sure that you administer the entire assessment. If your assessment and your child's performance do not match up, investigate possible causes such as test anxiety or lack of information.

BEYOND ACADEMICS

Well Planned Start is a great tool to help you discern your child's readiness for early learning skills. But, don't forget to let your child follow his natural interests through play.

Play during these early learning years is critical, as it establishes a framework for a love of learning and for the development of solid interests in coming years.

While learning games and educational toys are great resources during this time, free play is just as important. So, make a point to let free play time direct more of the day than academics or even structured play.

NUMBER RECOGNITION

	YES	NO
Can your child match a numeral with the same number of objects up to ten?	○	○
Can your child write the numbers up to ten?	○	○
Can your child finish a dot-to-dot picture up to ten?	○	○
Can your child count up to ten objects and write the correct number?	○	○

WHOLE AND PART

	YES	NO
Can your child divide a sandwich or apple into half?	○	○
Can your child put together a cut and paste project where the pieces make a whole?	○	○
Can your child put two groups of objects together and tell how many there are?	○	○
Can your child tell you the parts of a train or a doll?	○	○

COMPARING

	YES	NO
Can your child point to the smaller of two circles?	○	○
Can your child look at a group of 2 objects and a group of 4 objects and tell you which has more?	○	○
Can your child match up symmetrical sides or mirror images?	○	○
Can your child put shapes in order from smallest to largest?	○	○

ADDITION AND SUBTRACTION

	YES	NO
Can your child take 6 red objects and 3 blue objects and count how many there are in all?	○	○
Can your child start with 3 objects and add objects one at a time to reach 8?	○	○
Can your child start with 3 crackers, eat 2, and tell you how many are left?	○	○
Can your child take 10 objects, put 7 in a cup, and tell how many are left?	○	○

GRAPHING

	YES	NO
Can your child name two things that belong outside and two things that belong inside?	○	○
Can your child take a handful of candy, count how many of each color there are, and write the number?	○	○
Can your child line up 9 red objects, 5 blue objects, and 2 yellow objects and tell you which has the most and which has the least?	○	○
Can your child look at a chart of fruit, ask family members their favorites, and put a mark next to the correct ones?	○	○

Math

PreK - 1st grade

STARTING OUT
MATH

Math is one of the first activities many children get enthusiastic about. They feel a thrill as they learn to count, discover shapes in real life objects, and get to start actually writing in a "big kid" workbook!

Use math in daily life, incorporating counting, shapes, addition and subtraction, parts of a whole, and other such concepts into normal life activities.

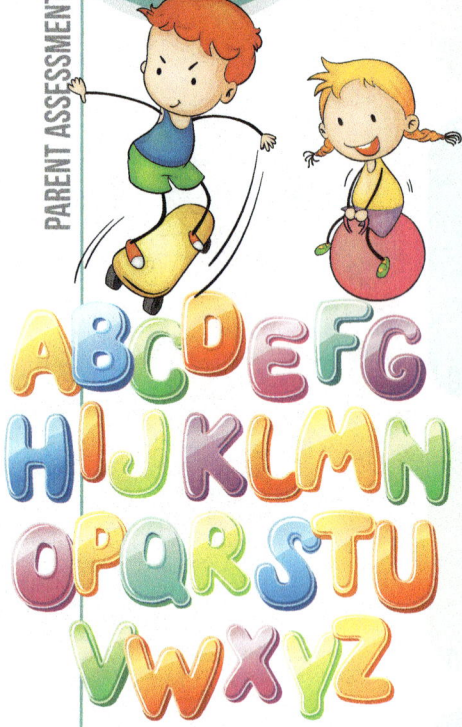

Language Arts

PreK - 1st grade
STARTING OUT
LANGUAGE ARTS

Oral language has been your child's world for his entire life. These early learning years allow you to introduce him to written language. This is the age for learning letters, their sounds, and how to write them.

Reading aloud is possibly the most integral part of this stage! Don't be afraid to read the same book again and again, knowing that repetition breeds learning.

LEARNING TO READ

	YES	NO
Does your child know that we read from left to right and from top to bottom?	○	○
Does your child recognize and know the names of some upper and lower case letters?	○	○
Does your child know that each letter has its own sound?	○	○
Does your child try to sound out words?	○	○

UNDERSTANDING A STORY

	YES	NO
Is your child able to tell what happened in a story?	○	○
Can your child guess what is next in a story?	○	○
Does your child understand that some stories are pretend and others can really happen?	○	○
Can your child follow verbal directions?	○	○

WRITING

	YES	NO
Can you read the letters that your child writes?	○	○
Can your child write his or her name?	○	○
Can your child write upper case letters?	○	○
Can your child write lower case letters?	○	○

SPELLING

	YES	NO
Does your child try to write messages?	○	○
Does your child ask you how to spell words?	○	○
Can your child sound out and spell simple words?	○	○
Can your child copy simple text?	○	○

LITERATURE

	YES	NO
Does your child understand that stories have beginnings, middles, and ends?	○	○
Does your child enjoy saying nursery rhymes?	○	○
Does your child enjoy being read to?	○	○
Is your child able to listen to short nonfiction selections about interesting things?	○	○

WORLD HISTORY

	YES	NO
Does your child have a basic understanding of a timeline?	○	○
Is your child able to tell you what things are "old-fashioned"?	○	○
Can your child tell you what things can happen today?	○	○
Does your child understand the cause and effect of different historical events?	○	○

WORLD GEOGRAPHY

	YES	NO
Does your child know what rivers, lakes, and mountains are?	○	○
Can your child locate the Atlantic and Pacific oceans?	○	○
Is your child able to tell you where the north and south poles are?	○	○
Can your child tell you where in the world one would find certain things?	○	○

UNITED STATES HISTORY

	YES	NO
Is your child familiar with Native American culture?	○	○
Can your child tell you who the Pilgrims were?	○	○
Does your child know who the first US President was?	○	○
Is your child familiar with symbols of our country?	○	○

UNITED STATES GEOGRAPHY

	YES	NO
Does your child know what city you live in?	○	○
Does your child know what state you live in?	○	○
Can your student locate the United States on a world map or globe?	○	○
Is your child able to find directions on a map?	○	○

CULTURE

	YES	NO
Can your child recognize the traditional clothing of different countries?	○	○
Does your child enjoy eating food from other countries?	○	○
Is your child aware that each country has its own games?	○	○
Can your child name holidays from around the world?	○	○

History
& Geography

PreK - 1st grade

STARTING OUT
HISTORY & GEOGRAPHY

There is little need for formal history learning right now. Instead, this stage is well suited to learning about people groups, cultures, and the idea that the way people live changes over the course of time.

Find read-alouds about missionaries, picture books about other cultures and time periods, and fun recipes from around the world and enjoy exploring!

Science

SPRING

SUMMER

AUTUMN

WINTER

PreK - 1st grade

STARTING OUT
SCIENCE

Formal science is not only unnecessary at this stage, it can also be counterproductive. Even so, scientific learning delights most children in this stage.

Let science be completely fun and hands-on during these early years. Find books with kid-friendly experiments, get out in the yard for nature exploration, and have fun getting your hands dirty.

PLANTS

	YES	NO
Does your child know what plants need to grow?	○	○
Can your child name the parts of a plant?	○	○
Is your child aware that plants make their own food?	○	○
Does you child understand that we get food from plants?	○	○

ANIMALS

	YES	NO
Can your child tell you what different animals eat?	○	○
Is your child able to tell where animals live?	○	○
Does your child know what kind of offspring different animals have?	○	○
Can your child tell you how to take care of pets?	○	○

HUMAN BODY

	YES	NO
Is your child able to tell you about each of the five senses?	○	○
Does your child understand healthy foods?	○	○
Can your child perform some of his or her own hygiene?	○	○
Is your child active?	○	○

SEASONS AND WEATHER

	YES	NO
Does your child know how seasons change nature?	○	○
Can your child describe different types of weather?	○	○
Is your child able to name outdoor activities for each season?	○	○
Can your child put the seasons in order?	○	○

GENERAL SCIENCE

	YES	NO
Does your child know what a magnet is?	○	○
Can your child tell what things require electricity?	○	○
Is your child able to tell how to use a lever, a wheel, and a ramp?	○	○
Does your child understand that some things are man-made?	○	○

BIBLE STORIES

	YES	NO
Does your child know the story of creation?	◯	◯
Can your child tell you who Abraham was?	◯	◯
Is your child familiar with the story of Noah?	◯	◯
Does your child know who Moses was?	◯	◯

BIBLE REFERENCE TOOLS

	YES	NO
Does your child know that the Bible is divided into the Old and New Testament?	◯	◯
Can your child name some Bible books?	◯	◯
Is your child able to find a chapter within a Bible book?	◯	◯
Does your child know how to find a verse within a chapter?	◯	◯

BIBLE PASSAGES

	YES	NO
Is your child familiar with Genesis 1:1? *In the beginning God created the heavens and the earth.*	◯	◯
Is your child familiar with 1 John 4:10? *This is love: not that we loved God, but that he loved us and sent his Son...*	◯	◯
Is your child familiar with John 1:29? *The next day John saw Jesus coming toward him and said, "Look, the Lamb of God...*	◯	◯
Is your child familiar with John 3:16? *For God so loved the world that he gave his one and only Son, that whoever believes...*	◯	◯

THEOLOGY

	YES	NO
Does your child understand that the Bible is the Word of God?	◯	◯
Can your child tell you about sin?	◯	◯
Is your child aware that salvation is through Jesus Christ?	◯	◯
Does your child understand that God is faithful?	◯	◯

CHURCH HISTORY & MISSIONS

	YES	NO
Does your child understand that Paul was a missionary?	◯	◯
Can your child tell you how the first churches were started?	◯	◯
Is your child familiar with what missionaries do?	◯	◯
Does your child know what missionaries your church supports?	◯	◯

PreK - 1st grade
STARTING OUT
BIBLE

This is an exciting stage in Bible teaching as your child engages in stories and picture books. Take advantage of that by reading aloud from Bible storybooks and picture books that introduce theological concepts.

Don't hesitate to also do some reading and memorization from a solid Bible translation. Even if your child cannot understand it all, he will get used to the language of Scripture.

MATH

Score	Section
	Number Recognition
	Whole & Part
	Comparing
	Addition & Subtraction
	Graphing

Total Score

Grade Placement

LANGUAGE ARTS

Score	Section
	Learning to Read
	Understanding a Story
	Writing
	Spelling
	Literature

Total Score

Grade Placement

HISTORY & GEOGRAPHY

Score	Section
	World History
	World Geography
	United States History
	United States Geography
	Culture

Total Score

Grade Placement

SCIENCE

Score	Section
	Plants
	Animals
	Human Body
	Seasons & Weather
	General Science

Total Score

Grade Placement

BIBLE

Score	Section
	Bible Stories
	Bible Reference Tools
	Bible Passages
	Theology
	Church History and Missions

Total Score

Grade Placement

PARENT ASSESSMENT SCORING

The Well Planned Start was designed to assess a grade level *per subject.* Use the key below to *determine the grade level for each subject.*

1. Count the number of questions you answered yes to in each section. Write the number in the score box to the left of the section.

2. Add the section scores together and place the total in the **Total Score** box.

3. Using the key below, determine the grade assessment for *each subject.*

SUBJECT TEST KEY

- Total Score = 20: Administer the 1st grade test for this subject. Your child may be ready for 2nd grade.
- Total Score = 15-19: Your child is ready for the 1st grade.
- Total Score = 10-14: Base your decision on the following **section scores.**
  - Score 2 or less in 1-2 sections: Your child is ready for the 1st grade in this subject, but you can expect to give extra help throughout the year.
  - Score 2 or less in 3-5 sections: Your child should begin this subject at a kindergarten level.
- All sections = 0-9: Lay a solid foundation for learning by focusing on the topics covered in this test.

BIBLE EXCEPTION

Because the development of spiritual growth is not confined to a grade level, the Bible tests for Well Planned Start were designed to cover a range through the following stages of education:

- Starting Out - Preschool - 1st Grade
- Getting Excited: 2nd - 4th Grade
- Beginning to Understand: 5th - 8th Grade
- Learning to Reason: 9th - 12th Grade

When scoring Bible and determining placement, it is recommended to use your discretion in deciding if additional testing is needed or more time studying the topics covered.

WHAT NEXT?

The parent assessment is a guide to what key information your child should know by the end of kindergarten. Once you have finished taking the assessment and scoring the results, you can proceed to give the student placement assessment to confirm your results.

Use this area to take notes about specific topics, subjects, and processes you feel your child will need help with. After your child has taken the placement test, compare your notes and the scores from the parent assessment to determine subject grades, overall grade level, and plan of action for the coming school year.

DETERMINING A
GRADE LEVEL

Assessment results can indicate grade levels below, at, or above kindergarten. If you homeschool, you can purchase grade specific curriculum for each subject. However, if you are looking for a means to determine an overall grade level, use the suggestions below in deciding.

- If your child scores above or below a kindergarten level in math or language arts, you can easily incorporate materials from the assessed grade level. Your child should school in the 1st grade.

- If you child scores below a kindergarten level in three or more subjects (math, history, science, and language arts), we recommend repeating kindergarten.

- If your child scores above a kindergarten level in three or more subjects (math, history, science, and language arts), we recommend testing with the 1st grade test for advanced placement.

- If your child scores ahead and behind in 2 or more subjects (math, history, science, and language arts), your child should school in the 1st grade.

- Reevaluate every year to be sure that your child is still at the correct grade.

#2 PROCEED

Proceed with Student Placement

STUDENT PLACEMENT TEST

The following pages contain the student placement tests for math, language arts, history and geography, science, and Bible. Along with the instructions on the test, there is also a section beginning on page 43 to reference as you watch your child work through the questions and answers. Utilizing this student placement test administrator guide will allow you to recognize the areas of struggle for your child and the point where problem solving breaks down.

The assessments ahead are a tool for you to use to better understand your child's academic needs. Here are a few more tips to use when administering these evaluations:

- Choose a calm day and a quiet space for assessment.

- Make sure your child is fresh and feeling well. Do not administer the assessments after three hours of calculus.

- Choose a time that is calm and fresh for you as well, as you will be working through the assessment with your child. It is important to minimize distractions for both you and your child during this time.

- Unless you have a child who enjoys tests and challenges, present these assessments as a new kind of activity or worksheet. If you say "test," they may lock up.

- Each assessment is printed on perforated pages. Simply remove each page and give it to the child to work on.

- Read the directions aloud and make sure your child understands them well.

- If the instructions are written in terms your child does not understand, feel free to change the wording.

- Take your time! These are not timed assessments. You are looking for correct thinking, not speed.

- As you process through this assessment with your child, go with your gut instinct. If you feel your child is good at something, say so. If you feel he or she is struggling, say so.

- Lack of information does not necessarily indicate a gap. For example, if you have not covered early American history yet but are sure your child would understand it, give your child credit for abilities.

- Look for creative thought processes. If you think an answer is weird, ask your child to explain how he or she arrived at it. If the logic behind the answer makes sense, give your child some credit.

- For concrete questions like math or science, watch for correct processes. Your child may be solving everything correctly and just writing down a wrong number or making a mistake in computation. If you are unsure, provide a new, similar problem for your child to work, or ask him to take another look. Having your child show his work will help.

- If you feel that there is a significant gap or that your child has not "gotten" the information after repeated exposure, please seek a professional evaluation for underlying issues. Whether you assign a label or not, understanding your child will make you a better teacher.

REMEMBER! ADMINISTRATOR GUIDE IS LOCATED BEHIND THE STUDENT TEST.

1. Circle the number that matches the number of objects.

4   8   9

10   8   12

1   3   5

2. Fill in the missing numbers.

1 ... 3 4 ... 7 ... 9 ...

3. Connect the dots to make a picture.

4. Count the objects and write the number.

Math

5.

Circle the picture that shows half.

a.

b.

6. What parts go together to make a whole?

a.

e.

b.

f.

c.

g.

d.

h.

7. Circle all the stars. How many are there?

8. Circle the things that go together.

a.

b.

c.

d.

e.

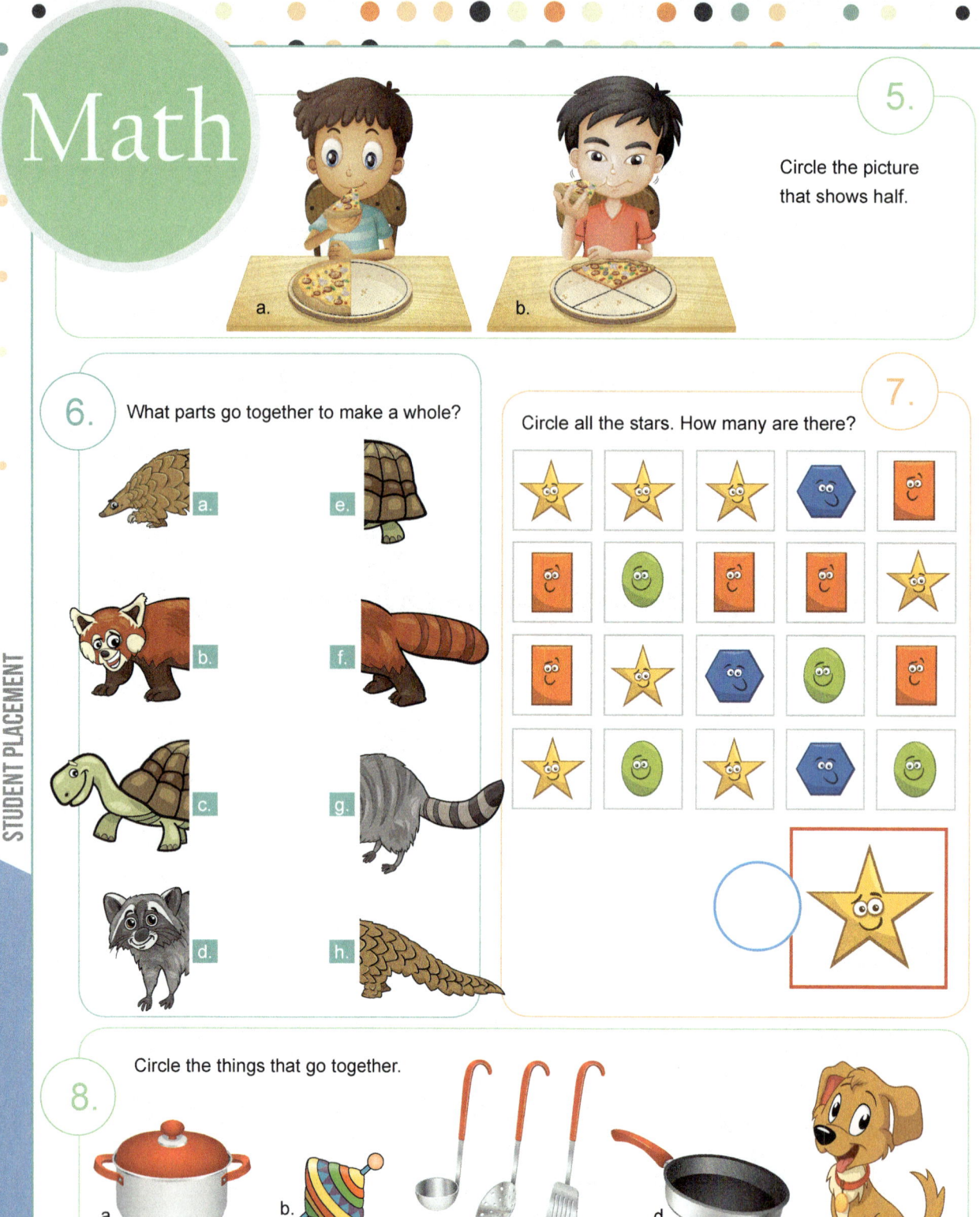

9. Which circle is smaller?

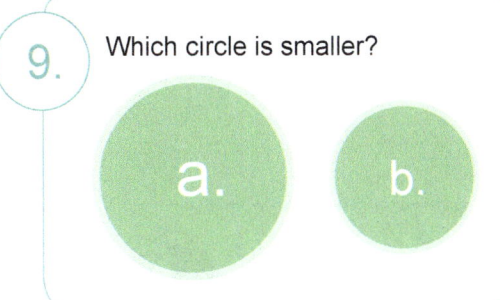

a.   b.

10. Which tree has more apples?

a.   b.

11. Circle the objects that are the same on both sides.

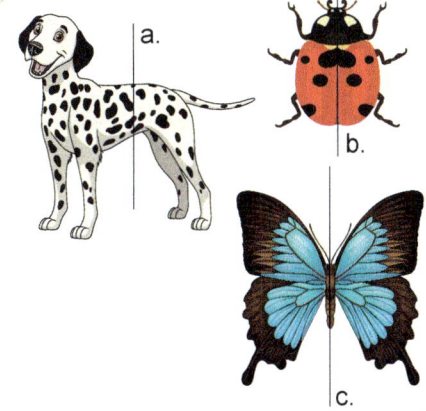

a.

b.

c.

12. Put the shapes in order from smallest to largest.

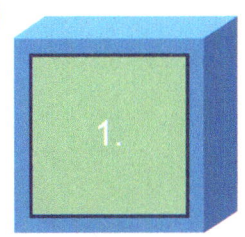

1.   2.   3.   4.

13. How many marbles?

14. If you have 3 oranges, circle how many more oranges you need to make 8.

15. If you have 3 crackers and eat 2 crackers, how many crackers do you have left?

17

Math

16. If you have 10 flowers and put 7 flowers in a vase, how many flowers do you have left?

17. Draw a line from each object to where you would find them.

Inside

Outside

18. Count how many of each object you can find and write the number in the circle below that object.

19. Look at the orange balls, green balls, and yellow balls. Circle the group with the most. Draw a box around the group with the least.

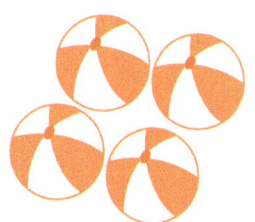  

20. Look at the chart of fruit. Ask your family their favorite kind and color in one box for each person.

	1	2	3	4

Language Arts

1. Trace the lines.

2. Match the upper case and lower case letters.

T	e
B	t
E	a
A	b

3. Circle the letter that each picture starts with.

B T R

S P L

H E B

Z I N

4. Read the words and draw a line to the picture.

a.

b.

c.

d.

cat   hen   pot   egg

5.

Look at these pictures. Circle who this story is about.

6.

a.   b. c.   d.

Circle the picture of what will happen next in this story.

7.

a.   b.   c. d.

Circle the picture of something that you might really see.

8. Follow your test administrator's instructions.

Language Arts

## 9

Copy these letters.

10.

Write your name.

STUDENT PLACEMENT

11.

Write the missing upper case letters.

a

b

c

d

e

12.

Write the missing lower case letters.

F

G

H

I

J

22

13. Circle the correct spelling.

she	seh
was	wuz
de	be
nto	not
their	thier

14. Circle the correct way to spell each picture.

jump	pump		fur	fir

black	back

brown	brow		blew	blue

15. Write the missing letters of the picture.

s____w

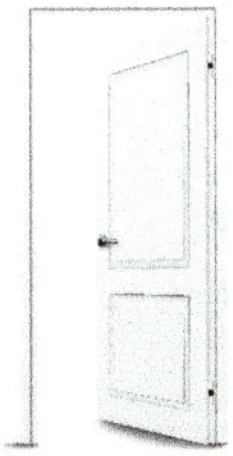

ope____

p____ny

r____d

____ellow

16. Copy this sentence.

The new girl is my friend now.

Language Arts

17. Put these pictures in order.

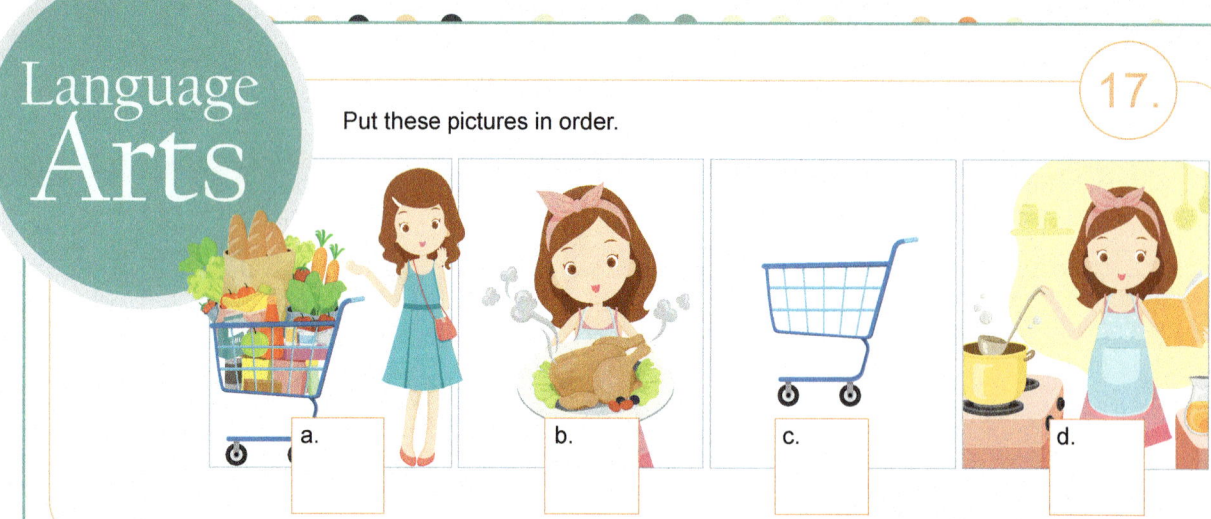

a. ☐ b. ☐ c. ☐ d. ☐

18. Say a nursery rhyme for your mom or dad.

19. Listen to your mom or dad read this.

Frog ran up the path to Toad's house.

He knocked on the front door.

There was no answer.

"Toad, Toad," shouted Frog, "wake up. It is spring!" "Blah," said a voice from inside the house.

"Toad, Toad," cried Frog.

Circle how this story made you feel.

20. Listen to your mom or dad read about insects.

Insects are small animals with six legs and a hard outer shell called an exoskeleton. Most insects have wings and antennae.

Circle the pictures of insects.

History
& Geography

1. Put the pictures in order from oldest to newest.

2. Draw a line to match the picture of what we use today with what people used long ago.

3. Circle the things that are common today.

swimming pool

wooden boats

tepee

pizza delivery

4. Match the pictures with important events in history.

a. United States Constitution   b. Thanksgiving   c. Continental Railroad

History

& Geography

5. In the image above, circle the river, underline the lake, and draw a box around the mountains.

6. On the globe to the left, put an X on the Atlantic Ocean and put a check on the Pacific Ocean.

7. On the globe to the left, draw an arrow on the North Pole and draw a star on the South Pole.

8. Draw a line from the picture to where it is in the world.

a.

b.

c.

d.

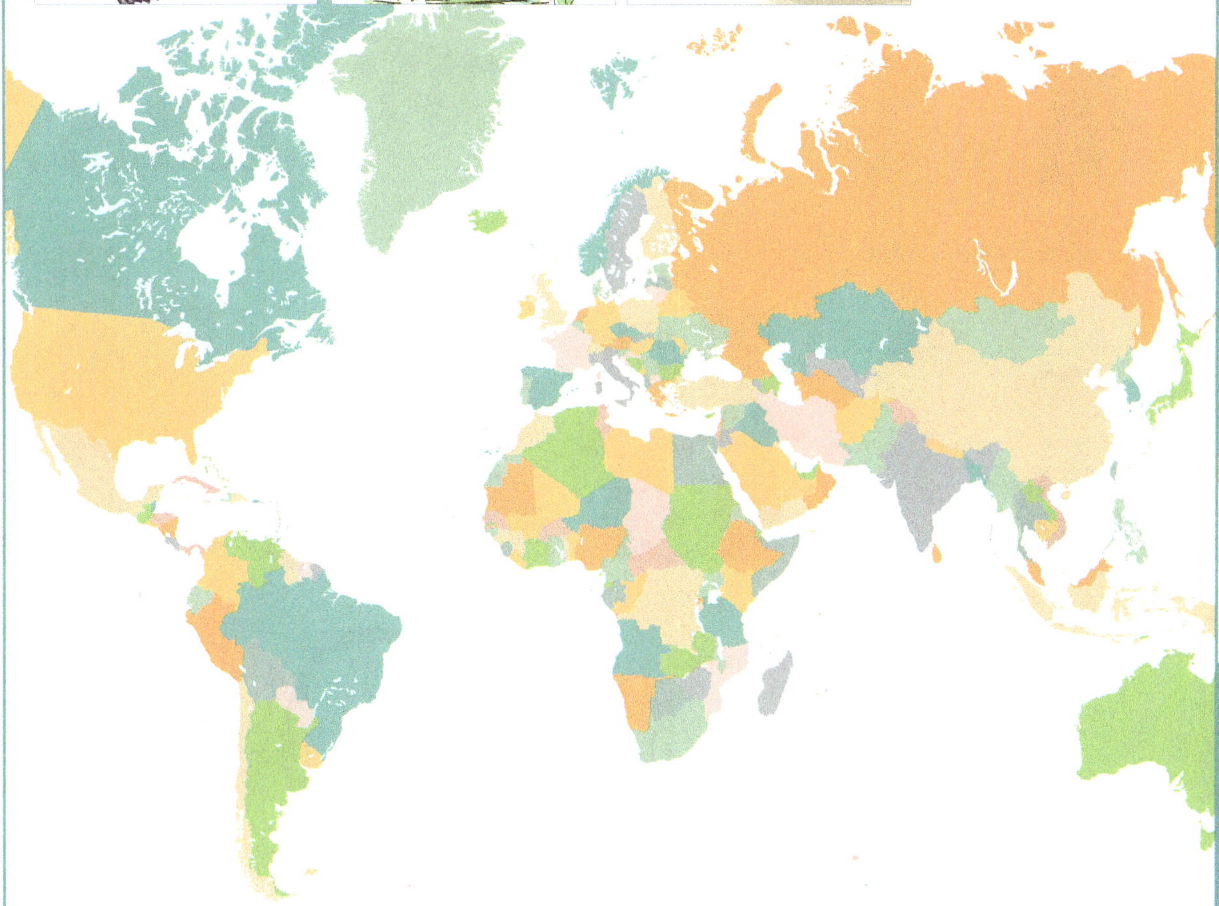

e.

f.

g.

9. Circle the things you would find in a Native American village.

a. b. c. d. e. f. g.

10. Circle the picture of the Pilgrim family.

a. b. c. d.

11. Draw a box around George Washington.

a. b. c.

12. Circle the symbols of the United States.

a. b. c. d. e.

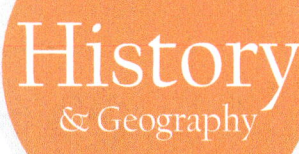

13. What city do you live in?

_____

— — — — — — — — — — — — — — — — —

_____

14. What state do you live in?

_____

— — — — — — — — — — — — — — — — —

_____

15. Draw a star on the United States.

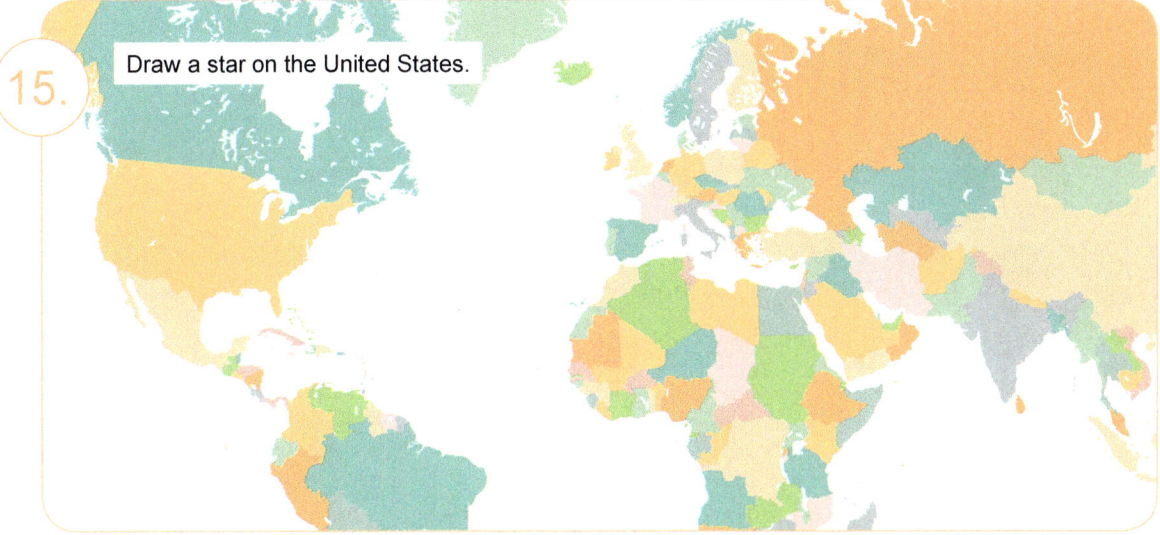

16. Put an X on the house that is East of the brown house.

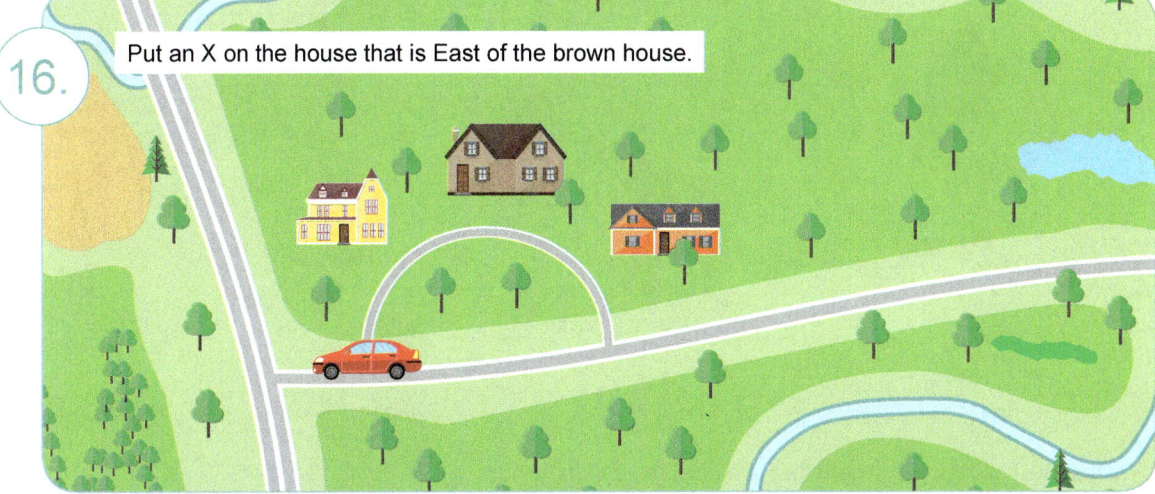

17.

Match the child with where he or she lives in the world.

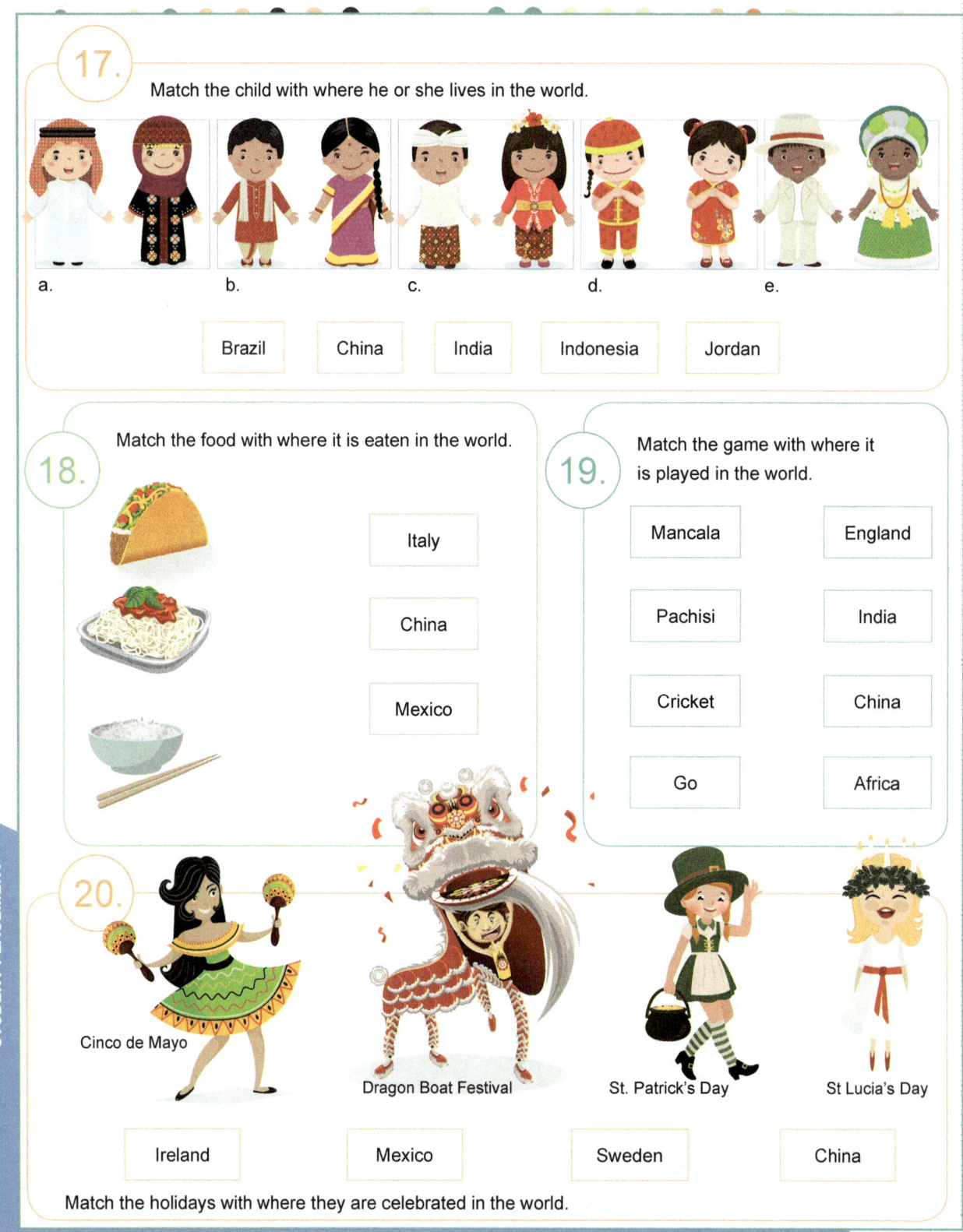

a.   b.   c.   d.   e.

| Brazil | China | India | Indonesia | Jordan |

18. Match the food with where it is eaten in the world.

| Italy |

| China |

| Mexico |

19. Match the game with where it is played in the world.

| Mancala | England |

| Pachisi | India |

| Cricket | China |

| Go | Africa |

20.

Cinco de Mayo

Dragon Boat Festival

St. Patrick's Day

St Lucia's Day

| Ireland | Mexico | Sweden | China |

Match the holidays with where they are celebrated in the world.

Science

1. Circle the things that plants need to grow.

2. Draw a line to match the parts of the plant.

stem

root

flower

leaves

fruit

3. Circle the part of the plant that makes food for the plant.

4. Draw a line from the food to the plant it comes from.

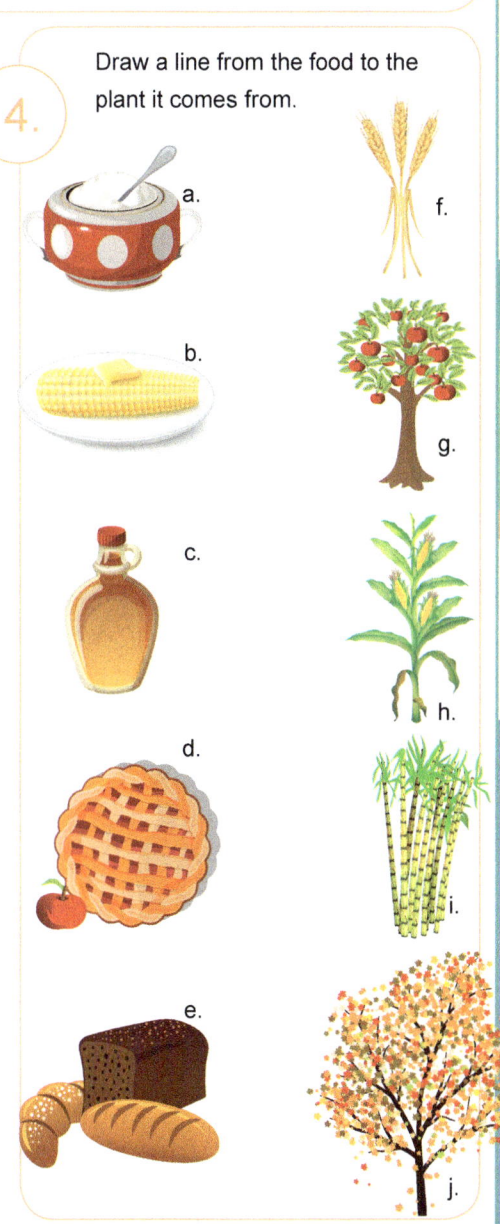

Science

5. Draw a line from the animal to its home.

- hive
- iceberg
- ocean
- den
- nest

6. Draw a line from the animal to the food it eats.

7. Circle ways that you can take care of pets.

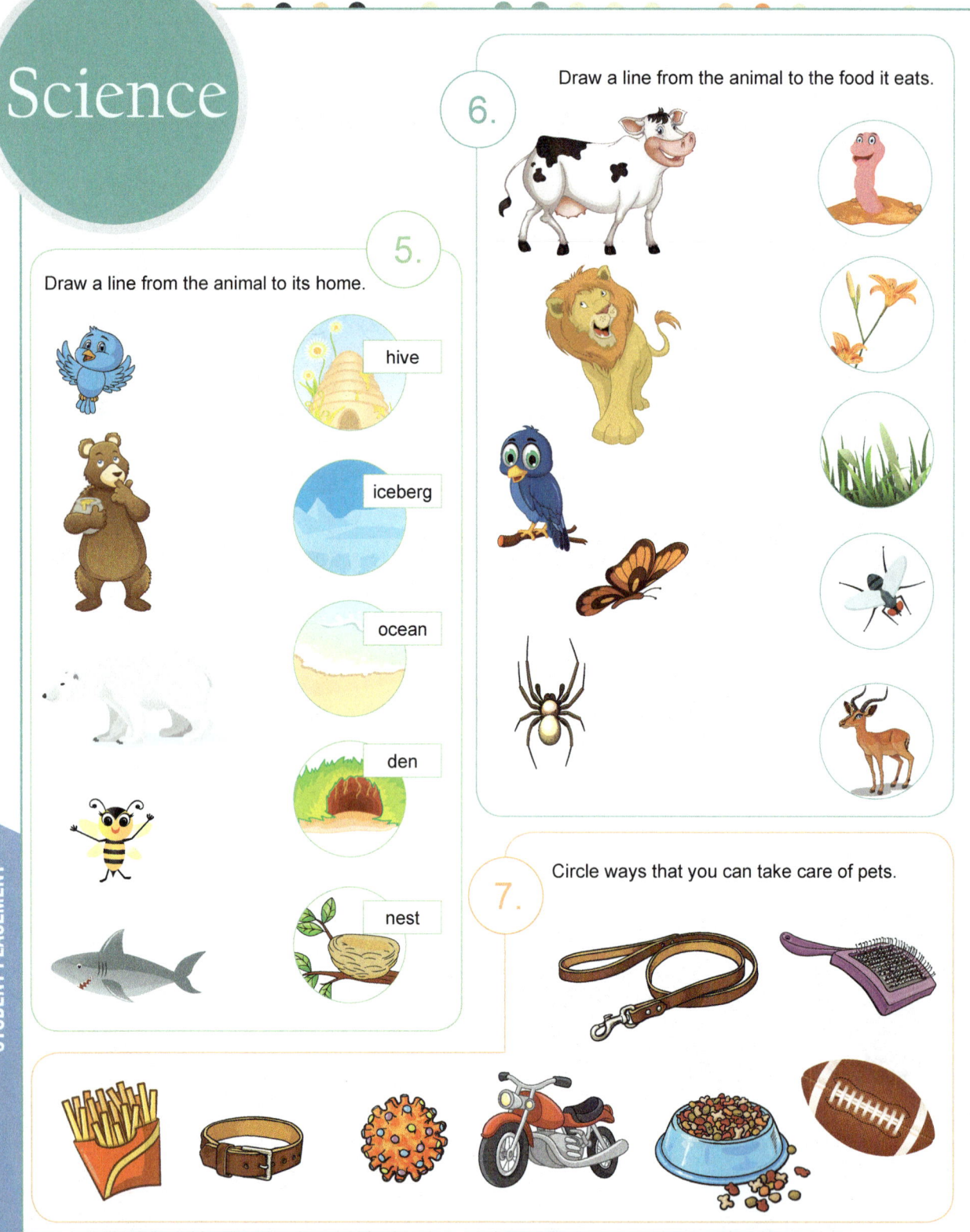

8. Match the animal with its baby.

9. Match the part of the body with the experience.

11. Match the body part with what we use to clean it.

10. Circle the healthy foods.

Science

12. Circle the ways to get exercise.

13. Match the weather with the clothing.

a.

b.

c.

14. Match the season with what happens in nature.

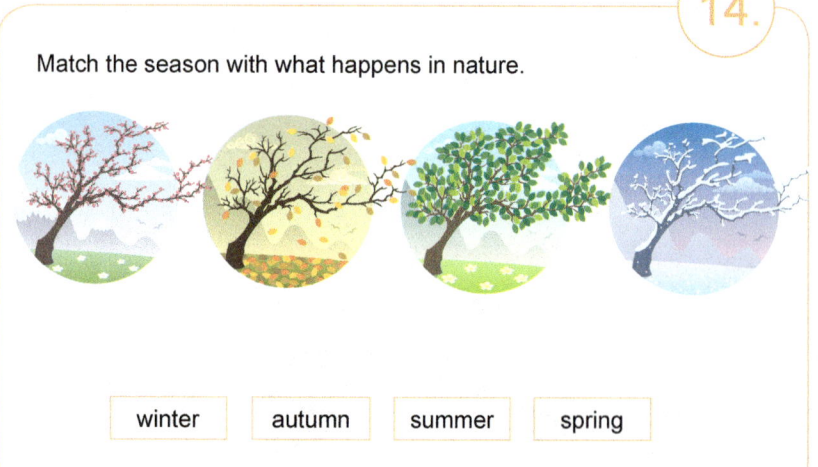

| winter | autumn | summer | spring |

15.

Draw a line from the weather to the activity.

a.

b.

c.

16.

Put the seasons in order starting with spring.

☐  SUMMER

☐  SPRING

☐  WINTER

☐  AUTUMN

17.

Circle the items that use electricity.

Science

Circle the objects that are magnetic.

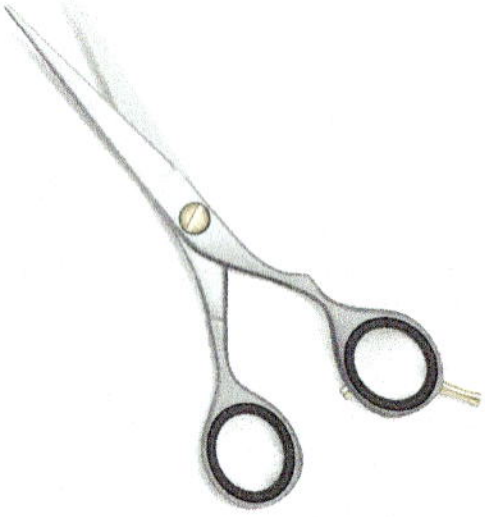

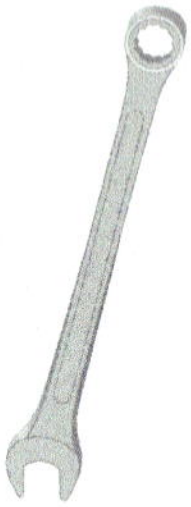

19. Match the simple machine with how it is used.

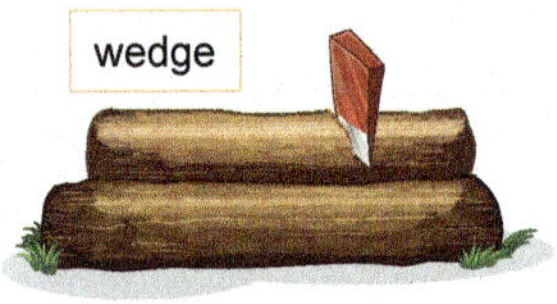

wedge

wheel

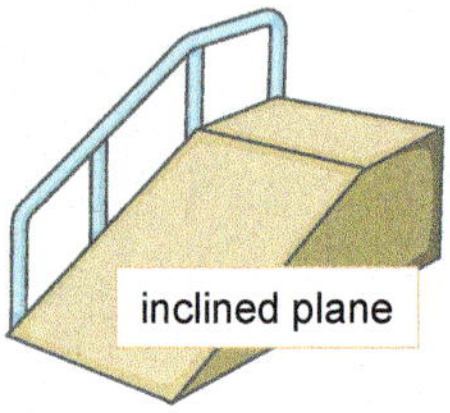

inclined plane

lever

| moving a load | lifting something | an axe cutting | a wheelchair ramp |

20. Circle the things that are man-made.

1. Match the days of Creation

Day 1

 land and plants

Day 2

 sea and flying creatures

Day 3

 light and dark

Day 4

 sun, moon, stars

Day 5

 land animals and man

Day 6

 clouds and ocean

2. Check the picture of Abraham

a.

b.

3. Name the Bible story.

Bible

4. Check the picture of Moses.

a.

b.

5. The Bible is divided into the _____ and _____.

a. Old Testament and New Testament

b. beginning and end

c. first part and second part

6. Circle the books of the Bible named after Bible story characters.

Esther

Genesis

Joshua

1 Kings

Job

Proverbs

Mark

Acts

1 Peter

Romans

1 John

1 Thessalonians

CHAPTER 1

1 There was a man in the land of Uz, ...ose name was Job; and that man was ...t and upright, and one that feared ...d eschewed evil.

...re were born unto him seven sons ...ghters.

...ce also was seven thousand ... thousand camels, and five ...en, and five hundred she ...eat household; so that ...est of all the men of ... feas

THE BOOK OF
JOB

6 Now there was a da... God came to present them... LORD, and Satan came also... 7 And the LORD said unto ... comest thou? Then Satan a... LORD, and said, from going to ... the earth, and from walking up an... it.

8 And the LORD ... thou considered ... none li...

7. In the Bible above, circle the chapter number.

8. In the Bible above, put a square around the verse number.

9. Fill in the blanks of Genesis 1:1 (NIV).

In the _____

God _____ the heavens

and the _____.

Bible

STUDENT PLACEMENT

10. Fill in the blanks of 1 John 4:10 (NIV).

This is _____: not that we loved _____,

but that he loved us and sent his _____ as an atoning

sacrifice for our _____.

11. Fill in the blanks of John 1:29.

The next day _____

saw Jesus coming toward him and said,

"Look, the _____

of God, who takes away the

_____ of the world!

12. Fill in the blanks of John 3:16

For _____ so loved the

_____ that he gave his one

and only _____, that who-

ever _____ in him shall

not _____ but have eternal

_____.

13. True or False:

The Bible is the Word of God.

14. Circle the examples of sin.

lying   playing a game

disobeying   praying

hugging   stealing

15. How do we go to heaven.

a. being a good person

b. trusting Jesus as our Savior

c. taking an elevator

Bibliotheca

16. Faithfulness means:

a. loyalty; staying true

b. an intense feeling of deep affection

c. happiness

17. The first churches were started by:

a. the Pharisees

b. the children of Israel

c. Christians who learned about Jesus from the Apostles

18.

a.

b.

Check the picture of Paul.

19. Circle what a missionary does.

build churches

serve people

make lots of money

start schools

share the gospel

works for the government

20. Where does your church send missionaries?

STUDENT PLACEMENT TEST ADMINISTRATOR GUIDE

In the following pages, you will find the student placement test administrator guide. This section walks you through assessing your child during the test and includes an answer key and scoring chart.

SECTIONS

Each subject test is divided into 5 sections. This allows you to break up the test as needed and evaluate based on both individual section scores and an overall subject score.

ASSESS

This column includes questions and information to help you understand the goal of the test question. Use these questions to help identify and assess knowledge of the subject matter or understanding of processes, whether or not your child answers correctly.

ANSWERS

This column indicates the correct answer for the questions. Occasionally this column is merged with the notes column to give ample room for detailed answer information.

NOTES

In order to help you understand how a child should arrive at an answer, we have included this section to give the details of the processes. As well, this area includes helpful tips on the goals for the question and how your child should arrive at answers.

✓ SCORES

Use this area to indicate a correct answer or sufficient knowledge to give credit for the question. Use either a checkmark or a number one. As your child completes each section, add up the marks and place the total in the "Section Score" box at the top of the section. These scores will be used to tally your child's subject and overall scores at the end of the test.

SUMMARY

The final page of this section is used to summarize the section scores, subject scores, and overall grade placement.

TEST HACKS

Combat test nervousness and reduce stress by utilizing some of these Test Hacks.

1. Prepare snacks in advance, including protein to munch on during the test and other snacks for break time.

2. When choosing a test location, consider where your child learns best, even if that means lounging in a hammock or sitting on an exercise ball.

3. Grab a stress ball, Silly Putty, gum, or other little tools to have on hand to combat fidgetiness.

4. If your child seems nervous, add in a little fun by periodically surprising them with a question like, "What is your favorite color?" or asking them to do something funny like draw a goofy alien with horns.

5. If you begin seeing signs of stress during the test, take a break to do jumping jacks, take 10 deep breaths, or go for a 15-minute walk or bike ride.

6. Diffusing a citrus oil like lemon, grapefruit, or orange is good to alleviate stress and improve focus without using overly calming scents like lavender.

PLACEMENT TEST GUIDE

Use when administering and scoring

Math

#	Assess	Answer	Notes	✔
NUMBER RECOGNITION			Section Score	
1	Does your child understand that a numeral represents a number of objects?	4,8,1		
2	Can your child write the numerals up to 10?	2; 5; 6; 8; 10		
3	Does your child understand that numbers have an order?	connecting dots in number order should result in a picture of a turtle		
4	Does your child understand the one-to-one concept of objects and numbers?	11; 3		
WHOLE & PART			Section Score	
5	Does your child understand that half is less than a whole?	a.		
6	Does your child understand that a whole is the sum of all its parts?	a;h b;f c;e d;g		
7	Can your child visually discriminate objects and count them?	7		
8	Can your child make associations between objects and actions?	a;c;d		
COMPARING			Section Score	
9	Does your child understand bigger and smaller?	b.		
10	Does your child understand more and less?	b.		
11	Does your child recognize when an object is the same on both sides or a mirror image?	b, c		
12	Is your child able to put given objects in order?	2,4,3,1		

Math

#	Assess	Answer	Notes	✔
ADDITION & SUBTRACTION			Section Score	
13	Does your child understand that combining groups of things makes one larger group?	9		
14	If your child is given a number, can he or she count up to another number?	5		
15	Does your child understand that taking some away from a group leaves a smaller group?	1		
16	Is your child able to count how many things are left when some are taken away?	3		
GRAPHING			Section Score	
17	Is your child able to sort objects?	inside - lamp, toy horse outside - cow, lawn mower		
18	Does your child understand how to count a certain type of object?	guitars - 7 books - 13 yarn - 8 hats - 4		
19	Can your child compare groups of objects?	circle - yellow balls box - green balls		
20	Is your child able to make a chart?	Answers will vary. Be sure your student counts the correct number of boxes.		

STUDENT PLACEMENT TEST GUIDE

#	Assess	Answer	Notes	✔
LEARNING TO READ			Section Score	
1	Does your child understand that we read and write from left to right and top to bottom?		Make sure your student is following the directions of the arrows.	
2	Is your child able to recognize some capital and lower case letters?		T-t B-b E-e A-a	
3	Can your child make some letter sounds?		T - Tree S - Sneaker B - Bucket I - Ice Cream	
4	Does your child make an effort to sound out 3-letter words?		cat - d. hen - a. pot - b. egg - c.	
UNDERSTANDING A STORY			Section Score	
5	Does your child understand that stories are about characters?		The main character is the girl cleaning the floor and sweeping.	
6	Does your child understand that events happen in an order?		d.	
7	Is your child beginning to understand the difference between fact and fiction?		c.	
8	Is your child able to follow simple instructions?		Give your child the following instructions: Put a circle around the square. Draw a line through the triangle. Put an check mark in the center of the circle.	
WRITING			Section Score	
9	Can your child copy the alphabet?		Make sure your student is forming the letters correctly.	
10	Can your child write his or her name?		Be sure your student begins his or her name with a capital letter and that it is spelled correctly.	
11	Can your child write upper case letters?		A B C D E	
12	Can your child write lower case letters?		f g h i j	

Language Arts

#	Assess	Answer	Notes	✔
SPELLING			Section Score	
13	Can your child sound out enough of a word to find its meaning?	she was be not their		
14	Does your child understand that letters must be in a certain order to make a word?	jump fir brown blue black		
15	Can your child sound out a word and guess which letter is missing?	a n o e y		
16	Can your child copy a sentence?	Does your student accurately spell each word, capitalize the first word, and add the period?		
LITERATURE			Section Score	
17	Does your child understand sequences?	c. a. d. b.		
18	Does your child enjoy saying things for Mom and Dad?	This can be any nursery rhyme of your student's choosing.		
19	Does your child have an emotional response to things you read?	There is no correct answer for this question. The goal is to give you insight into how much your student enjoys literature.		
20	Can your child gain information and facts by listening to you read?	ladybug cricket bee ant		

#	Assess	Answer	Notes	✓
WORLD HISTORY			Section Score	
1	Does your child recognize some things as old and other things as modern?	pyramids Viking ship knights wagon rocket		
2	Is your child aware that how we do things has changed over the course of time?	washboard - washing machine car - wagon letter - typewriter		
3	Does your child understand that some ways of doing things are no longer used?	swimming pool pizza delivery		
4	Does your child have a basic understanding of the order of history?	c. a. b.		
WORLD GEOGRAPHY			Section Score	
5	Does your child know some basic landforms?			
6	Does your child know the names of some of the oceans?			
7	Does your child understand some basic directions?			
8	Does your child understand that people, places, and things are different around the world?	a. Penguin - the southern tip of South America or the Antarctica region b. Eiffel Tower - Europe c. Lion - Africa d. Great Wall - Asia e. Bald Eagle - North America f. Christ the Redeemer - South America g. Kangaroos - Australia		

#	Assess	Answer	Notes	✔
UNITED STATES HISTORY			Section Score	
9	Is your child familiar with Native American culture?	a. Indian headdress b. wigwam c. tepee f. canoe		
10	Does your child know that some of the first settlers were called Pilgrims?	c.		
11	Is your child familiar with George Washington?	b.		
12	Does your child recognize some national symbols?	a. Statue of Liberty c. Flag e. White House		
UNITED STATES GEOGRAPHY			Section Score	
13	Does your student know what a city or town is?	Answers will vary.		
14	Does your child know what a state is?	Answers will vary.		
15	Does your child know what a country is?			
16	Can your child use a compass rose on a map?			
CULTURE			Section Score	
17	Does your child know how people from different countries live?	a. - Jordan b. - India c. - Indonesia d. - China e. - Brazil		
18	Does your child know that people around the world eat different things?	rice - China tacos - Mexico spaghetti - Italy		
19	Does your child understand that people around the world enjoy different things?	cricket - England pachisi - India go - China mancala - Africa		
20	Is your child aware that people around the world celebrate different things?	Cinco de Mayo - Mexico Dragon Boat Festival - China St. Patrick's Day - Ireland St. Lucia's Day - Sweden		

STUDENT PLACEMENT TEST GUIDE

#	Assess	Answer	Notes	✔
PLANTS			Section Score	
1	Does your child understand that water, soil, light, and air are necessary for plant growth?	water sunlight soil		
2	Does your child know stem, leaf, flower, and root?	a. root b. stem c. flower d. fruit e. leaves	The stem supports the leaves, fruit, and flowers. The roots are below the ground. The flowers are white and yellow. The leaves are flat with jagged edges. The tomatoes are the fruit.	
3	Does your child understand that plants make their own food?	Leaves make food for the plant by photosynthesis. However your student might circle the roots because they gather nutrients and sometimes store food. Discuss his or her reasoning.		
4	Does your child know that we get food from plants?	a. sugar - i. sugar cane b. ear of corn - h. corn stalks c. maple syrup - j. maple tree d. apple pie - g. apple tree e. breads - f. wheat sheaves		
ANIMALS			Section Score	
5	Does your child know that animals live in different places?	bird - nest bear - den polar bear - iceberg bee - hive shark - ocean		
6	Does your child know that some animals eat plants and others eat meat?	cow - grass lion - gazelle bird - worm butterfly - flower spider - insects		
7	Does your child understand that we should take care of animals?	leash brush collar toy ball bowl of food		
8	Is your child aware of animals and their young?	cat - kitten kangaroo - joey horse - colt frog - tadpoles owl - owlet		
HUMAN BODY			Section Score	
9	Does your child know that our senses gather information for us?	ear - bell hand - campfire eye - picture mouth - apple		

#	Assess	Answer	Notes	✔
10	Does your child understand the difference between healthy food and junk food?	orange carrot whole grain bread milk fish		
11	Does your child understand basic hygiene?	hair - brush teeth - toothbrush face - washcloth		
12	Is your child aware that physical activity keeps us healthy?	go on a hike walk the dog ride a bicycle jump rope roller skate		
SEASONS & WEATHER			Section Score	
13	Does your child understand different types of weather?	a. rainy b. sunny c. snowy		
14	Does your child observe seasonal changes?	Season pictures from left to right: spring, autumn, summer, winter		
15	Does your child know that certain activities are only done in certain types of weather?	a. snowy b. rainy c. sunny		
16	Does your child understand the cycle of seasons?	2 1 4 3		
GENERAL SCIENCE			Section Score	
17	Does your child understand that electricity powers things?	toaster light bulb TV		
18	Does your child know that magnets attract things?	safety pin scissors twrench		
19	Can your child explain how to use ramps, wheels, and levers?	wheel - moving a load lever - lifting something wedge - an axe cutting inclined plane - a wheelchair ramp		
20	Does your child know the difference between man-made objects and natural objects?	bottle car building		

STUDENT PLACEMENT TEST GUIDE

#	Assess	Answer	✔
BIBLE STORIES		Section Score	
1	Does your child talk about all the things God has made?	Day 1 - light and dark Day 2 - clouds and ocean Day 3 - land and plants Day 4 - sun, moon, stars Day 5 - sea and flying creatures Day 6 - land animals and man	
2	Does your child talk about Abraham, Isaac, and Jacob?	b	
3	Does your child talk about Noah and the Flood?	Noah & the Ark	
4	Does your child talk about Moses, Pharaoh, and the children of Israel?	a.	
BIBLE REFERENCE TOOLS		Section Score	
5	Does your child take an interest when you open your Bible?	a.	
6	Does your child attempt to find books of the Bible?	Esther Joshua Job Mark 1 Peter 1 John	
7	Does your child show an understanding that chapters and verses are in numerical order?		
8	Does your child attempt to find and read verses?		

#	Assess	Answer	✔
BIBLE PASSAGES		Section Score	
9	Does your child know that God made the heavens and the earth?	beginning, created, earth	
10	Does your child know that God loves us?	love, God, Son, sin	
11	Does your child know that Jesus is the Lamb of God?	John, Lamb, sin	
12	Does your child know that God sent His Son?	God, world, Son, believes, perish, life	
THEOLOGY		Section Score	
13	Does your child display a respect for the Word of God?	True	
14	Does your child show that he or she knows what is right and wrong?	lying disobeying stealing	
15	Does your child ask questions about what happens after we die?	b.	
16	Does your child want to talk to God?	a.	
CHURCH HISTORY AND MISSIONS		Section Score	
17	Does your child talk about God and Jesus?	c.	
18	Is your child interested in missionary stories?	b.	
19	Does your child want to help others?	build churches serve people start schools share the gospel	
20	Does your child take an interest in other countries and cultures?	Answers will vary.	

Notes

MATH

Score | Section
- Number Recognition
- Whole & Part
- Comparing
- Addition & Subtraction
- Graphing

Total Score

Grade Placement

LANGUAGE ARTS

Score | Section
- Learning to Read
- Understanding a Story
- Writing
- Spelling
- Literature

Total Score

Grade Placement

HISTORY & GEOGRAPHY

Score | Section
- World History
- World Geography
- United States History
- United States Geography
- Culture

Total Score

Grade Placement

SCIENCE

Score | Section
- Plants
- Animals
- Human Body
- Seasons & Weather
- General Science

Total Score

Grade Placement

BIBLE

Score | Section
- Bible Stories
- Bible Reference Tools
- Bible Passages
- Theology
- Church History and Missions

Total Score

Grade Placement

STUDENT PLACEMENT SCORING

The Well Planned Start was designed to assess a grade level *per subject.* Use the key below to *determine the grade level for each subject.*

1. Each correct answer is valued at 1 point. Count the number in each section. Write the number in the score box to the left of the section.

2. Add the section scores together and place the total in the **Total Score** box.

3. Using the key below, determine the grade assessment for *each subject.*

SUBJECT TEST KEY

- Total Score = 20: Administer the 1st grade test for this subject. Your child may be ready for 2nd grade.
- Total Score = 15-19: Your child is ready for the 1st grade.
- Total Score = 10-14: Base your decision on the following **section scores.**
  - Score 2 or less in 1-2 sections: Your child is ready for the 1st grade in this subject, but you can expect to give extra help throughout the year.
  - Score 2 or less in 3-5 sections: Your child should begin this subject at a kindergarten level.
- All sections = 0-9: Lay a solid foundation for learning by focusing on the topics covered in this test.

BIBLE EXCEPTION

Because the development of spiritual growth is not confined to a grade level, the Bible tests for Well Planned Start were designed to cover a range through the following stages of education:

- Starting Out - Preschool - 1st Grade
- Getting Exciting: 2nd - 4th Grade
- Beginning to Understand: 5th - 8th Grade
- Learning to Reason: 9th - 12th Grade

When scoring Bible and determining placement, it is recommended to use your discretion in deciding if additional testing is needed or more time studying the topics covered.

WHAT NEXT?

Compare your findings to the parent assessment test and begin to make a plan of action on the following page.

If you suspect a learning challenge or special needs, we strongly recommend additional testing with a specialist.

MATH

grade

_____
_____
_____
_____
_____
_____
_____

LANGUAGE ARTS

grade

_____
_____
_____
_____
_____
_____
_____

HISTORY & GEOGRAPHY

grade

_____
_____
_____
_____
_____
_____
_____

SCICNCE

_____
_____
_____
_____
_____
_____
_____

BIBLE

_____
_____
_____
_____
_____
_____
_____

PLAN OF ACTION

Your child has completed the test, the scores are tallied, and a grade level is determined. But, it doesn't stop there! Here are some ways to utilize the information gleaned from this assessment to help you and your child tackle the new school year with confidence!

HOMESCHOOL

Use this space to note your child's grade level, gaps you observed during testing, areas where your child excels, and specific strategies you will be seeking as you choose curriculum. Make a list of academic needs for the coming year, and have that list on hand to check against the content in your curricula of choice.

HYBRIDS: CO-OP, TUTORIAL, & ENRICHMENTS

If your child is involved in homeschool classes taught through a co-op, use this area to note learning needs to discuss with your child's teacher(s). Also, make note of any enrichment activities you can do with your child to fill in gaps and strengthen weaknesses.

TRADITIONAL SCHOOL

If your child attends a private or public school, make note of areas you want to discuss with your child's teacher(s) to determine how to strengthen weaknesses. At home, plan trips or organize evening discussion to cater to strengths and incorporate Bible training.

STAGES OF EDUCATION (PREK - 1ST GRADE)
STARTING OUT

We've all heard it said that young minds are like sponges, and the saying is indeed true. Little ones take in an abundant amount of information, beginning even before birth. By the time they reach first or second grade, this absorption learning begins to morph into a great enthusiasm and excitement about academics. But, in order to reach that excitement, we must remember to fill the early learning years with tools that our children need to prepare for learning. This is the time to let our children explore, gather, accumulate, and absorb as much as possible in fun, exciting ways.

When we let our early learners absorb without weighing them down with heavily structured learning, it may feel as if we are neglecting academic development that will get them ahead in future years. But the opposite is actually true. We are actually equipping them, laying a foundation that will allow them to truly enjoy the more formal learning that is to come.

1. Provide information in a variety of ways. Look for bugs and plant life while playing in the backyard. Explore books, books, and more books. Play games. In the process, use "real" words. Call spiders arachnids and let children memorize entire verses of Scripture instead of modified child-friendly versions. Keep information age-appropriate, but do not back down from challenging information.

2. Read and read some more. Reading aloud together is a great relational activity that also instills a love of books. If your child learns now that books are beautiful, then there will be no limit to the fountain of understanding later in life.

3. Observe. Because your precious young learner is learning naturally, this is the perfect time to watch for learning styles to reveal themselves. Does your child pour over picture books or does he prefer to hear a story read aloud? Does she constantly move while learning something new? Does music help him focus better? By observing these patterns now, you will be able to tailor future academics to fit your child's learning styles.

4. As you process through this stage, consider it to be an opportunity to store up building blocks for later usage.

PARENT
TEACHING TIPS

In the following pages you will find practical teaching tips and activity suggestions for every concept covered in the placement test. Here are some ways to utilize these tips:

1. Use the suggested activities to strengthen low-scoring areas.

2. For strong areas, focus on activities that will keep your child challenged.

3. At times, having a negative experience with academics can take the joy out of learning. Restore that joy gently by choosing activities that will be fun for your child.

4. Use enrichment activities to put together a "summer camp." This is the perfect time to fill in gaps and bring kids up to grade level.

5. If you are homeschooling, utilize some of these activities on days that are too interrupted or chaotic for the normal school schedule. You can also use them for a relaxed "Friday Fun Day!"

6. Liven up a co-op class by incorporating some of these activities.

PARENT TEACHING TIPS

To use throughout the entire year!

Math

NUMBER RECOGNITION

- Play a board game that involves counting.
- Use bingo daubers to create patterns for your child to finish.
- Play bingo.
- Practice drawing a given number of objects.
- String beads or Froot Loops. Be sure to count and create patterns.

WHOLE & PART

- Cut shapes from paper and allow your child to cut them in half.
- Set up a store and let your child use pennies to purchase things.
- Get a fun math workbook or print some math worksheets.
- Let an older sibling help your little one with math work.
- Invest in some puzzles.

GRAPHING

- Have your child sort colored candies and tell how many there are of each color.
- Create a bar graph and show your child how to graph sorted objects.
- Do a survey of favorite cookies and show your child how to write tally marks to count up the preferences.

COMPARING

- Give your child a mixture of objects and allow him or her to sort them into muffin tins.
- Buy some shape cookie cutters and use them for cookies or stencils.
- Give your child some measuring cups and have him or her arrange them in order. Then allow some free play with rice or water.
- Invest in a balance scale to compare objects.
- Measure the length of something with random objects such as pencils, paper clips, or blocks.

ADDITION & SUBTRACTION

- Do addition and subtraction problems with small pieces of candy.
- Count everything from plates while setting the table to washcloths while folding laundry.
- Let your child help you divide treats up for himself and his siblings.
- Find something for your child to look for and count while driving.

JOURNAL YOUR EFFORTS

If you feel that your child is extremely behind, consider formal testing for a learning difficulty such as dyscalculia.

Language Arts

JOURNAL YOUR EFFORTS

LEARNING TO READ

- Get your child his or her very own library card and use it.
- Read out loud to your child.
- Let your child look at books any time he or she wants.
- Allow your child to read in bed for a few minutes before lights out.
- Read some rebus books.

UNDERSTANDING A STORY

- Encourage your child to draw pictures of stories he or she has heard or made up.
- Let your child look at the pictures of a story and tell you what is happening.
- Set up a reading circle of stuffed animals and let your child "read" to them.
- Provide dress up clothes for imaginative play.
- Ask your child to tell you about a book he or she is looking at.

WRITING

- Look for objects that rhyme.
- Let your child practice writing letters in shaving cream.
- Create textured letter cards.
- Encourage tracing and drawing to develop fine motor skills.
- Print some worksheets or get a workbook for extra practice.

SPELLING

- Get some letter board games.
- Go on a scavenger hunt for "b" words.
- Get some letter puzzles or tiles and practice making words.
- While riding in the car, look for letters.

LITERATURE

- Let your child choose his or her own library books.
- Memorize some nursery rhymes or poems.
- Read more than just fiction. Throw some factual pieces in there too.
- Ask your children's librarian for a book list.
- Attend library programs.

If you feel that your child is extremely behind, consider formal testing for a learning difficulty such as dyslexia or dysgraphia.

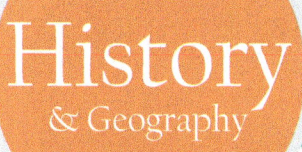

History
& Geography

WORLD HISTORY

- Read some picture books about famous people.
- Go to a museum.
- Get a subscription to a history or geography magazine.
- Read about the countries your ancestors came from.
- Make a family tree.

WORLD GEOGRAPHY

- Get a globe.
- Use map puzzles to introduce geography.
- Anytime you read about a place, find it on the map or globe.

CULTURE

- Help your child find biographies of a favorite person.
- Create a family story book with personal stories.
- Find an interesting bit of international news and share it with your child.
- Watch some period movies.
- Try food from other countries.

UNITED STATES HISTORY

- Teach the Pledge of Allegiance and the national anthem.
- Visit local historical sites.
- Take a guided tour of something.
- Take your children to the voting locations and government buildings and explain why you are there.

UNITED STATES GEOGRAPHY

- Make it a point to visit some historical locations and museums on vacation.
- Explain holidays to your child.
- Make a family time capsule.
- Create a timeline with pictures.
- Print coloring pages of famous people, places, and events.

JOURNAL YOUR EFFORTS

Science

PLANTS

- Identify the types of plants around your home.
- Create a mystery box with different nature items.
- Get a subscription to a nature magazine.
- Plant a garden or some potted plants.
- Set aside a shelf for nature finds to be displayed.

JOURNAL YOUR EFFORTS

ANIMALS

- Point out different animals in your neighborhood.
- Get books from the library about animals.
- Get a pet.
- Provide a notebook and some drawing pencils to sketch nature pictures.
- Visit the zoo, nature center, or botanical garden.

HUMAN BODY

- Find various models of body parts, including the eye, heart, etc.
- Check the library for a five senses experiment book.
- Create a daily hygiene sticker chart.
- Start a family exercise routine.

SEASONS & WEATHER

- Print some season coloring pages.
- Visit a science museum.
- Check the weather together.
- Talk about seasonal changes.
- Make or buy a weather station for observation.

GENERAL SCIENCE

- Provide a magnifying glass.
- Provide a magnet play set.
- Let your child play with levers, wheels, and ramps.
- Gather some man-made and natural objects and have your child sort them.
- When your child asks a question, show him or her how to find the answer.

Bible

BIBLE STORIES

- Get a good Bible story book and read from it regularly.
- Read Bible stories in order.
- Start a Bible timeline.

BIBLE REFERENCE TOOLS

- Show your child your Bible.
- Give your child a Bible of his or her own.
- Practice finding verses together.

BIBLE PASSAGES

- Read Bible passages out loud.
- Read the same Bible passages over and over.
- Choose a verse of the year, month, or week. Say it every day.

THEOLOGY

- Talk to your child about God every day.
- Teach your child to listen respectfully when the Bible is read.
- Let your child know that you sin. Apologize when you sin against him or her.
- Tell the Christmas story and the Easter story every year.
- When your child expresses a need or desire, teach him or her to pray for it. Share how God has answered your prayers.

CHURCH HISTORY & MISSIONS

- Read about Paul's missionary journeys.
- Read the book of acts.
- Choose a missionary to study.
- Study the countries where your church's missionaries are serving.

MILESTONES
WHAT TO EXPECT

The timely development of a child is a frequent question and concern among both new and experienced parents. In the following pages you will discover the physical, emotional, and academic development you can expect from your child **by the end of kindergarten.**

The goal of the Well Planned Gal milestones is to have the information on hand as a guideline. These ranges of development can greatly aid you as you parent, teach, and train your child to the next level.

It is important, however, that you do not use these milestones to "diagnose" your child as behind or gifted. It is perfectly normal for children to display a broad range of abilities as they grow and develop.

Many things may influence a child's growth and development, including temporary stress, nutrition, illness, sleep habits, premature birth, learning styles, and physical growth spurts. If you have specific concerns or questions concerning your child's physical or academic progress, we urge you to consult your child's pediatrician.

The Well Planned Gal milestones are outlined in three ranges of growth and maturity.

YOUR CHILD SHOULD BE ABLE TO . . .

This area presents what **most** children this age are comfortable doing. Approximately 80% of children fall into this category.

YOUR CHILD MAY BE ABLE TO . . .

This area presents what **many** children this age are comfortable doing. Approximately 50% of children fall into this category.

YOUR CHILD MAY EVEN TRY TO . . .

This area presents what **some** children this age attempt. Approximately 20% of children -- including gifted or exceptional children -- fall into this category.

USING MILESTONES

What can your early learner do physically? What academic milestones should you expect during the preschool, kindergarten, and first grade years? How does your child grow emotionally during this stage?

Because every child is unique, any list of milestones should be understood as a general guide to what your child may be learning and doing during the Starting Out years, covering children ranging in age from three to seven.

The most important thing to remember is that the early years are a time of tremendous growth physically, emotionally, and mentally. This stage offers a valuable opportunity for your child to grow and explore at his own rate. "Book learning" will come soon enough, but these precious years pass too quickly. So, as you encourage development of these physical, emotional, and academic milestones, remember to do so through structured and free play more than any other avenue.

K MILESTONES

Understanding your child's growth

HOW YOUR CHILD IS GROWING

Date	✔	Milestone	Journal
Your child should be able to			
	☐	Jump on one foot	
	☐	Do somersaults	
	☐	Cut paper	
	☐	Print some letters and copy shapes	
	☐	Begin to lose teeth	
	☐	Use a fork and spoon correctly	
	☐	Care for himself in the restroom with no help	
Your child may be able to			
	☐	Swing by himself	
	☐	Enjoy vigorous play	
	☐	Bounce and catch a ball	
	☐	Skip using alternating feet	
	☐	Copy a diamond	
	☐	Distinguish his right hand from his left	
	☐	Draw a stick figure or face	
	☐	Tie his own shoes	
Your child may even be able to			
	☐	Write his own name	
	☐	Swim	
	☐	Jump rope	
	☐	Draw a person with twelve parts	
	☐	Throw and kick a ball well	
	☐	Play organized sports	

HOW YOUR CHILD IS GROWING

Date	✓	Milestone	Journal
	☐	Use measuring tools (ruler, measuring cups)	
	☐	Hold a pencil correctly	
	☐	Speak consonant blends correctly	
How you can help. You can encourage his growth through these milestones with activities like these:			
	☐	Take frequent visits to playground or park.	
	☐	Provide paper, scissors, crayons, and other art supplies.	
	☐	Encourage your child to trace shapes and letters and try to copy them.	
	☐	Hold him or her responsible for personal hygiene.	
	☐	Use right and left often in conversation with gestures to define direction.	
	☐	Consider joining a recreational sports team.	
	☐	Correct pronunciation occasionally and gently, asking him or her to repeat words correctly.	

Notes

HOW YOUR CHILD IS FEELING

Date	✓	Milestone	Journal
Your child should			
	☐	Know right from wrong	
	☐	Pretend	
	☐	Desire praise	
	☐	Imitate adults	
	☐	Want to play with others but prefer to play with friends of the same gender	
	☐	Conform to group behavior and notice when someone is not conforming	
	☐	Express anger verbally (rather than only physically)	
	☐	Express pride and embarrassment	
	☐	Begin organizing his friends in playing pretend or games	
Your child may			
	☐	Need affection from authority figures	
	☐	Sometimes be unkind to others	
	☐	Demonstrate a strong desire to win	
	☐	Take things personally	
	☐	Become inflexible	
	☐	Show awareness of others' feelings	
Your child may even			
	☐	Desire perfection	

HOW YOUR CHILD IS FEELING

Date	✓	Milestone	Journal
	☐	Worry more	
	☐	Have strong reactions	
	☐	Follow directions well	
	☐	Need less correction	
	☐	Accept defeat	
	☐	Take turns kindly	
	☐	Experience guilt	
	☐	Stay focused on one activity for increasing periods of time	
How you can help. You can encourage his growth through these milestones with activities like these:			
	☐	Provide frequent play time with children of various ages.	
	☐	State clear house rules.	
	☐	Help your child learn to "use words" when angry or frustrated.	
	☐	Praise him or her liberally.	
	☐	Avoid shaming him or her publicly.	
	☐	Provide dress-up clothes and props for pretend play.	
	☐	Coach him or her on appropriate responses to losing games.	
	☐	Help your child consider his or her friend's point of view.	

Notes

HOW YOUR CHILD IS LEARNING

Date	✓	Milestone	Journal
Your child should			
	☐	Write some letters and attempt to write his or her own name	
	☐	Know some letter sounds	
	☐	Repeat a story with several details,	
	☐	Understand the concepts of time (morning, afternoon, evening, night) and order daily activities in the correct time period (nap in the afternoon, supper in the evening)	
	☐	Understand spatial relationships (under, behind, past)	
	☐	Tell jokes	
	☐	Speak in sentences of six words or longer	
	☐	Count up to 10 objects	
	☐	Correctly name four colors and three shapes	
	☐	Memorize his or her address and phone number	
	☐	Enjoy being read to and pretend to read his favorite books	
	☐	Become very curious about nature	
Your child may			
	☐	Understand cause and effect	
	☐	Begin to write words	
	☐	Rhyme words	
	☐	Enjoy telling riddles or jokes and always find own jokes funny	

HOW YOUR CHILD IS LEARNING

Date	✓	Milestone	Journal
	☐	Understand opposites	
	☐	Identify a number of letters, sounds, and blends	
	☐	Read simple one-vowel words with help	
Your child may even			
	☐	Understand hours, minutes, seconds, months, days, weeks, and seasons	
	☐	Begin to exhibit a specific learning style	
	☐	Solve simple math problems	
	☐	Read a simple book aloud	
	☐	Recognize a significant number of sight words	
	☐	Decode basic phonics sounds and blends	
	☐	Speak and understand a broad vocabulary and use multi-syllable words	
	☐	Correctly use past and present verb tenses when speaking	
	☐	Answer "who, what, when, where, why" questions about events or stories	
How you can help. You can encourage his growth through these milestones with activities like these:			
	☐	Provide wide-lined paper and pencils for writing practice.	
	☐	Encourage letter tracing and recognition of own written name.	